Acknowledgments

(Front cover design 'Deepand Meaningful' by Sue Martin.)
Grateful thanks are due to the following ....
Jeremy Froy of J.I. Froy Computer Consultancy. Barton-le Clay, Beds. for computer advice
Martin McDonald of McDonald Repro. for printing expertise
Also to Sue Martin and Jane Plowman for editorial assistance
Benartex Inc., U.S.A., for providing some of their lovely fabric for me to use in many of the samples shown in this book
Clover MFG. Co Ltd. Japan., for samples of their wonderful metallic Quick Bias tape ... once again used in projects contained in this book
In addition special thanks are due to Nora Field, Alison King, Sue Martin, Kathleen McMahon, Jane Plowman, Carmen Redler and Mary Rich for agreeing to trial my patterns and allowing their work to be photographed.

Celtic Reflections

Why Celtic Reflections ?

it's all done by mirrors ....

and favours a bit of glitz provided by .... shiny fabrics ...

reflective beads ... and metallic Quick Bias and threads.

'Celtic Reflections' ...... © Angela Madden
ISBN   0 952 1060 8 6
First edition June 2001

M.C.Q. Publications.
Old Barn Cottage.
Luton Rd. Kimpton.
Herts. U.K.
SG4 8HA.

Distribution in U.S.A.
Quilters' Resource Inc.
P.O. Box 148850.
Chicago. Illinois 60614.
312 278 5795.

Distributor in New Zealand.
Margaret Barrett Distributors.
19, Beasley Ave.
P.O. Box 12 - 034
Penrose. Auckland.

Index

Page.

Also included .... master pattern sheet of Celtic designs.

Celtic cords and symbolic creatures

Celtic designs are truly timeless. First seen several hundred years before Christ, they are still popular today well over 2,000 years later. To their creators they were not just surface decoration but were deeply symbolic. Since their designers had no written language for many centuries, and tradition and culture were passed down through verbal means only ...... the full meaning of these patterns has retained its mystery.

The first designs were made up entirely of interlaced cords ... having no beginning or end .... purely abstract patterns. Applied to jewellery or clothing it is likely that their purpose was to act as magical protection for the wearer. The interweaving of the cords is thought to signify many things ... the in and out of breathing ... ceaseless movement .... the continuity of life .... and eternity.

The coming of Christianity led to the inclusion of religious figures and crosses. Celtic myths and legends provide clues to the significance of other representational images which are also seen, especially in the later manuscripts. Many were animals. Chickens, geese, rabbits, birds, dogs and fish are found in the Book of Kells.

Dogs were symbolic of the instinctual nature of man ... seen as protectors ... friends ... companions of heroes and gods in Celtic mythology

Swans represented solar deities .... healing powers ..... compassion .... sincerity and love. They were a favourite form of shape changer. The story of Caer ...... a beautiful fairy who lived in the form of a swan until she was wooed into human form by Aonghus Og, the god of love ... and that of the beautiful children of Lir ... cursed by their jealous stepmother Aoife, who turned them into swans for 900 years with only their wonderful singing for consolation, are well known examples of this common theme.

Birds are portrayed many times in old manuscripts. They were the messengers of the gods and bearers of good tidings. They too symbolised transformation and the ability to change shape. Celtic heroes often transformed themselves into birds and were therefore enabled to fly to foreign lands to avoid danger. The goose was a bird of Heaven and associated with the gods of war ... therefore becoming a symbol of power.

Whilst birds represented air ... and animals represented earth ... **fish** were also included to represent water. 'The salmon of knowledge' was said to live in a vast river whose waters were infused with wisdom. It was caught by the legendary hero Fionn Mac Cumhall who burnt his finger touching it whilst cooking. He sucked the finger and immediately became wise.

Celtic manuscripts were original to the style of the creators whilst reflecting the influences and methods of their time. The same can be said for many of the quilts stitched today. Many more animals than those mentioned above have personal significance for quilters and their families. With this in mind I have tried both to simplify and speed up design and stitching methods ...... and also update and widen the number and style of animals in the provided patterns.

The designs created from the instructions in this book need not be too deeply symbolic .... they can be made purely for fun. For whatever reason they are made, I sincerely hope they are enjoyed by both maker and user.

<u>Requirements for creating Celtic designs</u>

1. **Master Celtic patterns** ...... also butterflies, birds and beastie patterns ... all from this book.
2. **Thin tracing paper** ..... (or greaseproof paper).
3. **A pencil** .... (I prefer mechanical pencils.....they draw fine lines.)
4. **A medium tipped black felt pen.**
5. **A soft eraser.**
6. **Hinged mirror** ..... an essential design tool which enables you to see the full potential of each developing design. The ideal size is around 6 ins high x 12 ins long
(Light-weight unbreakable acrylic mirrors are now available . For designing full sized quilts two of these mirrors , straightened out and combined together as one double sized hinged mirror can be invaluable. (I find the 6 in square mirrors sold in quilt shops are too small to be useful for this technique, and framed mirrors obscure the view.)
7. **'BluTack' plastic adhesive.**
8. **Rotary cutting board.**

(If experiencing difficulty finding any of the branded requirements in U.S.A. please contact ......
Quilter's Resource Inc. P.O. Box 148850. Chicago, IL 60614. Tel 1-773-278-5695)

Requirements for needleworking designs

1. **An embroidery transfer pencil or pen** .... enables design to be marked on fabric by ironing.
2. **Rotary cutter.**
3. **Rotary cutting board.**
4. **Rotary cutting ruler** ...... with a 45° angle marked on it.
5. **Small sharp scissors.**
6. **Freezer paper.**
7. **Sewing machine** ...... capable of doing zig zag stitching.
8. **Size 60 machine needles.**
9. **Transparent thread** ...... 'clear' for light fabrics... 'smoke' for darks.
10. **Decorative threads** ...... (optional).
11. **Fabrics.**
12. **Quick Bias** ... (optional ...... creates a different look).
13. **Paper- backed fusible webbing** ...... (I favour Bondaweb, also called Wonder Under or Vliesofix .... other brands prevent stretch in the bias cut fabric necessary for completing designs.)
14. **Firm surfaced ironing board** ...... or covered board cut for this purpose.
15. **Non-stick ironing sheet** ...... prevents the fusible webbing sticking to either iron or board.

How to use this book

You will find there are four separate sections ....

1. Pages 7 - 41 contain instructions for designing, assembling and stitching.
The techniques described do not require any special artistic or needlework skills.
The instructions will provide a fast, easy route to creating your own original designs whether you are a complete beginner .... or an accomplished needleworker.
Several new techniques are described ..... extending Celtic needlework possibilities and achieving a new look.

2. Pages 42 - 79 provide patterns for a varied selection of butterflies, birds, and 'beasties'
which can be combined with Celtic cord patterns. The earliest Celtic manuscripts did not combine any representational images with cords. These patterns, more appropriately called 'interlace' or 'knotwork', were originally banned by the Christian Church in the 4th Century A.D. for being 'atheistic art'. However in the following centuries the Church apparently had a change of heart and 'Christianised' Celtic patterns by adding crosses, saints and various beasts .... many of which were mythical. This evolution of design can be seen to continue in later manuscripts ..... I have merely continued the process and taken the liberty of adding modern beasties more suited to the projects and tastes of the 21st Century.

3. Pages 80 - 94 showcase colour examples using the techniques described.
Many are examples of the first time the makers have tried these techniques. They are provided to inspire and spark your imagination. However, the fun part of using these methods is in creating designs which are original to each individual designer, suited to their own taste and requirements. There are no right or wrong designs ... the only question you should ask yourself is 'Do I like it?' If the answer is 'Yes' then go for it ...... if not ..... change it ..... or do another which you do like.

4. Finally inside the back cover is a large pull-out sheet containing cord patterns.
With the hinged mirrors it is easily possible to create a kaleidoscopic effect, stimulating the imagination and effortlessly providing the designer with endless variations in pattern size, shape and configuration.

Both the pattern sections can be photocopied or traced for use. The size can be altered to suit individual projects. Once copied all surplus paper around individual design sections should be cut away to prevent parts of neighbouring designs being obscured when they are used in combination.

Copying the patterns is a 'once only' task ...... it can be done at one go .... or gradually ......
you only need one or two design sections to begin having fun!

The complete collection provides a library of possibilities. The Celtic cords can be used on their own ... or they can be combined with butterflies, birds or beasties .... as you wish.

Most important of all ... use this book to have fun ....

If sewing isn't fun ..... why do it?

Celtic Design......
the fast easy way !

If you do not wish to cut the pattern sheet you can trace ..... or photocopy, the individual sections of Celtic knotwork.
It is possible to start designing with just one or two patterns .....
but having all 26 cut and ready to go will considerably increase the possibilities ...
and fun !
Heavier weight tracing paper is easier to handle than flimsy. Iron paper to flatten any wrinkles or curly edges.

Carefully cut the individual sections of knotwork apart.

Cut close to the outside edge of each section removing all surplus paper.

This enables sections to be positioned in close proximity without obscuring parts of each other.

The hinged mirror enables multiple views of a pattern to be seen at once.

Using a cutting board as a base allows the mirror to be accurately aligned to form a right angle at the hinge showing a multiple view which exactly matches the required finished size.

e.g. ..... positioning the mirror so that it borders a 10 in. square on the board will reflect a finished 20 in. size viewing area.

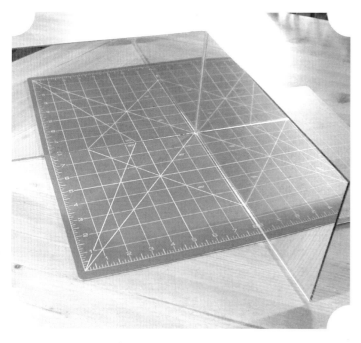

Paper design sections can be laid on the board within the 10 in. space ... and moved around until a pleasing design develops.

The use of a single design section creates an instant symmetrical pattern in four quarters.

The same section could be positioned in many different ways. Each time the overall pattern would change, producing instant variety.

The paper section can lie at a distance from ....
or touch ......
or underlap the base of either mirror.
Once again these alternatives create diversity and choice.

If you wish, only one side of the mirror can be viewed. It will stand up with the hinge flipped the opposite way around.

Now double- sided patterns can be auditioned.

Several design sections can be used at once.

Pattern possibilities are truly endless ....
and effortless!

All you have to do is play with alternatives until you find one that you like.

Original Celtic style designs with great charm and complexity can be achieved in seconds.

(Do not let the complexity of the design frighten you ... or limit your possibilities.
The assembly and stitching methods which follow are also the fastest and easiest ever!)

If design sections underlap the mirror, it is vital to check that the cord patterns can be clearly understood where the two views meet.

You should be able to see complete cords which flow without interruption from one view to the other.

The cords pictured left are correct.

If the mirror stands in the middle of a cord the cords will not look correct. Extra shapes will appear and confuse the pattern.
An example of this is the pointed oval at the base of the mirror in the middle of this picture.

If this is seen to be the case, it is easily put right .... there are two solutions ....

1. Ignore the extra shape .... if it were not there the cord pattern could be understood.

2. Move the mirror ... or ... the paper slightly until the cord pattern corrects itself.

Butterflies, birds or beasties can be added as you choose.

Having the chosen animal copied onto firm paper ... with the edges trimmed in the same way as the cords, makes designing easy.

They can be positioned in different ways... overlapping parts of the cord design as shown left .....which is very much in keeping with traditional designs ....

or freestanding.

When you are satisfied with the design ..... anchor the papers in their chosen position by pressing them on to tiny pieces of BluTack.

BluTack pieces should be big enough to stabilise the papers and prevent movement ....

but small enough to be pressed flat ... so as not to hinder the tracing at the next stage.

When the design is fixed in place, lay tracing paper on top. Anchor this in place in the same way .... with BluTack.
The piece of tracing paper must completely cover the exposed design.
It could be one sheet of paper of the right size with the edges touching the mirrors. Pictured right, it would be exactly one quarter of the completed design.

Alternatively, the tracing paper could be twice or four times as big ...
so that the entire design could fit onto it.
In these cases it should be folded into half or quarters, placing the mirrors on the folds.

Sections will fit together easily if lines are drawn along the folds at the base of the mirror.

When the tracing paper is anchored in place carefully move the mirror out of the way and trace the design exactly as you see it.

The remaining sections needed to complete the design can now be traced. Remove the BluTac from the tracing paper and trace another half / quarter of the design.

If you wish to create a large design it is not necessary to find tracing paper big enough to take the entire design. It can be transferred to the fabric in stages using quarters or halves.

Of course it is not compulsory to include multiples of the same animal in designs as per previous examples.

You might prefer not to include beasties at all. Patterns can look great made from cords alone .

Or .... if you cannot decide ...

complete the cord pattern first ... then audition alternative beasties in various positions to help with decision making.

Beasties placed asymmetrically .....
 or ....
mixing different species ...
might provide the look you prefer.

When a design is completed it is a good idea to establish how many cords you have created.

Each supplied pattern section contains only one cord. Run a finger around one as if driving a car along a road to confirm this.

However, by underlapping a mirror this can change. (Check out the heart shaped cord at the mirror's edge on the top of page 9.)

Lightly use coloured pencils to establish the path of each cord and to confirm how many are contained in your current design.
You may choose to use different fabrics for different cords.

Experimenting with Shape

Using this simple method of designing, it is possible to build up different shaped patterns.

Pictured right is a Christmas tree.
The completed design is shown on page 81.

The paper sections have just been placed beside each other as a half design, moving them around until the desired shape is achieved.

Both mirrors have been positioned in a straight line to reflect the other half.

Here a different style tree has been created using the same method.

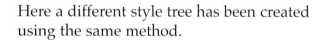

or here a heart .....

leaving a central space in which a chosen animal could have pride of place.

Joining Cords

Designs can be made up of individual design papers placed next to each other (as in the trees).

It is also easy to link one to another creating long continuous cord patterns which travel throughout the whole of a design.

Any point or corner on one piece of paper can be joined to any point or corner on another by placing one on top of the other.

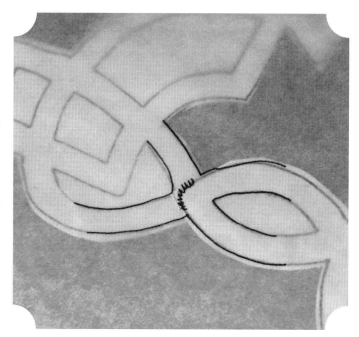

The outside and inside outline of each cord can then be traced as usual ...

(the only part omitted is the extreme point tip of the top paper which overlaps the other cord ... crossed out in the picture.)

The cords will now appear to flow smoothly from one section to the other.

This simple design trick will create apparently complex, flowing patterns ... but with no increase in design or sewing difficulty.

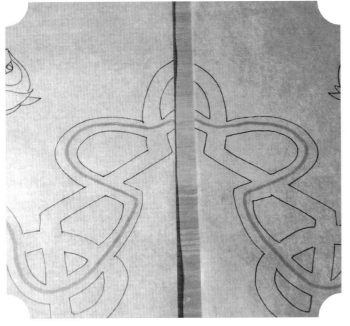

Sometimes cords can look awkward at the folds between mirrored sections. This can be fixed by moving the mirror .... but this might adversely affect another pleasant part of the design. It is possible to alter the course of cords crossing these folds.

Knowing that this can be done can sometimes be helpful in simplifying the route of a cord.

Cords can pass straight across a fold travelling into the neighbouring section ....
as pictured left ....

or ..... as pictured below ......

they can be turned back on themselves creating a loop which prevents them from entering the neighbouring section.
In this case the little peak which crosses the fold would be omitted.

Be sure to make all such alterations <u>before</u> the 'overs and unders' of the interlacing are marked. Then there will not be a problem.

The outlined shapes of the designs are symmetrical, exact mirror images of each other. However ..... the 'overs and unders' are not.

They will be opposite in adjoining sections.

To mark correctly interlaced 'overs and unders' <u>always begin by using pencil</u> which is erasable.

Think of your task as creating bridges which carry the cord 'roads' over each other.

Travelling along any road ..... two short straight lines are marked at each intersection where roads cross ....   e.g. **=** or **ǁ**
The only rules are ...
always go straight ahead at each crossing
and ....
the road being marked passes alternately over and under all others it crosses throughout the design.
Mark all 'overs and unders' on the whole design before going to the next stage ... fabric!

14

Transferring Designs to Fabric

Using the embroidery transfer pencil or pen ... draw a single line along the centre of each cord throughout the design. Heavily drawing this line will allow multiple transfers to be made.

Every time you come to an 'over' cord barring your way stop ....
and begin again on the other side.

This will transfer a single line design to your fabric which is easy to read ...
a continuous line through a crossing means that is an 'over' cord .....
whilst a broken line signifies an 'under' cord.

The animals will not be transferred... instead they will later be appliquéd in the blank spaces between the cords.

Select a piece of fabric which is larger than the drawn design ... (they always look better with space around the outside ... and if you don't like it , it can be cut off later.)

If you are using a quartered design .....
fold the fabric into four ...pressing the folds and therefore establishing the centre point.
If your design is a halved one ...
press the fabric in half.

These folds will help align the design correctly.
(They are the positions of the original mirrors.)

Use the folds as a visual guide to correctly position the design paper ... transfer pencil side next to the fabric.
Pin the design paper to the fabric. The picture shows a single quarter design
Press the design to transfer the pattern ...
using an iron which is hot enough to melt the transfer pencil ....
but not to scorch your paper or fabric.
Carefully remove one pin at a time   thoroughly checking that the transfer is complete..
 if not .... replace the pin and press again.

Do not remove the paper until absolutely
certain that the transfer is clearly visible.

In a quartered design opposite quarters are identical ..... but rotated through 180^0.

This enables an immediate repeat transfer to be made.

The paper is rotated, positioned and pinned against the folds in the same way.

Before the remaining two opposite quarters can be transferred the 'overs and unders' need to be reversed to transfer correctly.

This is not difficult to do.

Flip the tracing to the reverse side and using a coloured pen or pencil mark new bridges at every cord crossing.
(Use a new colour to avoid confusion.)

These should be marked going the opposite way to the previous bridges .... which can be seen through the paper.
i.e. ...... every 'over' becomes an 'under' and vice versa.

With the new bridges in place, it is easy to mark the centre line throughout the cord pattern as before.

Once again draw heavily with the transfer pencil to facilitate repeated transfers.

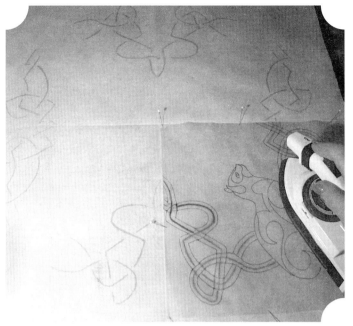

Both of the remaining quarters can now be transferred as before .....

using the folds as a placement guide ...

and checking that the 'cut' ends of the transferred cords match at the folds.

This completes the cord pattern ...
leaving spaces in which the animals can be placed.

If you have decided to mark a cord pattern first and think about animals later ... it will not matter that there are no blank spaces left after the transferring is completed.

Here is a design in which all the cords have been sewn down ... the decision to add animals has been deferred so that the final effect can be more clearly judged (see finished item inside front cover.)
Animals can be added anywhere over cords.
No extra bulk will be created by this overlap as once the outside edge of the creature has been stitched in place the background fabric will be cut away ...... (whether it contains cords or not) so everything will be returned to being one fabric layer throughout.

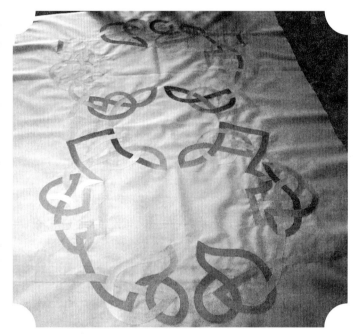

Transfer pencils or pens are made in several colours. However, some may not mark clearly enough on very dark fabrics.

These need a special white transfer pen ....
or ....
place the pattern under the fabric on a light box and mark the line using a white ....
or chalk pencil .... or dressmaker's carbon paper.

Here the white path the metallic cords are travelling along can be clearly seen against the very dark background.

Cutting Bias Cords

It is necessary to cut fabric on the bias
(i.e. ... at 45° to the warp and weft) for the cords.
If cut on the straight of the grain they would not travel neatly around the bends.
The cords will have 'raw edges' which will be first fused ... then stitched down.
As they are cut on the bias they will not fray.
It is not possible to give precise fabric amounts as every design is different ....
the rule is always over-estimate, don't be mean.
You will get approx 319 in. length of bias ... cut at 1/2 in.width from 1/8th yd. cut across the roll ....laying a piece of thread around the design cords will help to estimate your needs.

Cut an estimated square / rectangle of fabric.
Iron a same sized piece of Bondaweb (paper side up) to the **wrong** side of the fabric using a non stick ironing sheet underneath.
Trim one fabric edge parallel to the threads.

Align the 45° line on your rotary cutting ruler precisely with this edge ....

Rotary cut through both paper and fabric alongside the ruler.

(The cut does not have to run from corner to corner.)

Continue cutting at this angle producing strips at your required width.

The patterns provided can be completed with 1/4 in .... 3/8 in or 1/2 in wide bias.

(A wider width than these would require considerable enlargement of the patterns provided. Wider bias is also more difficult to take neatly around tight curves.)

Leave the backing paper in place on each strip until just before fusing it to the design.

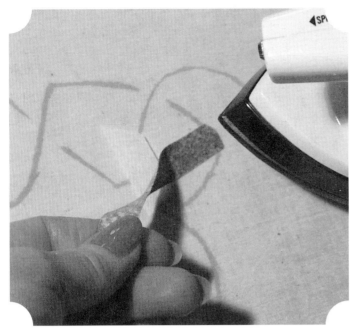

Fusing Bias Cords

Remove the backing paper from the first fabric strip, **but do not throw it away.**

<u>Always</u> begin fusing a cord half way through a gap that indicates an under crossing. You can end cords in the same position ..... (the 'over' cord will hide the joins.) .... or at points.
Set the iron at warm rather than hot.
Trim the cord start to match the marked 'over' line.
Tear off a short piece of your saved backing paper and place it under the fused cord at each 'over' crossing. This will facilitate the later placement of the 'under' cord which passes beneath.

At first the cord will just run around the design as there are as yet no cords to cross .... (unless it happens to cross itself).

Always remember to place the short pieces of backing paper under the cord every time it is the over cord (shown by a continuous line).
If you forget, it may be necessary to remove and replace a piece of bias as trying to lift it after it is fused can damage the edges.

On reaching a point cut across the cord and fuse in line with ... but slightly beyond the transfer mark ..... as pictured.
(The exception to this is when using Quick Bias when a mitre should be folded and not cut to achieve the neatest finish.)

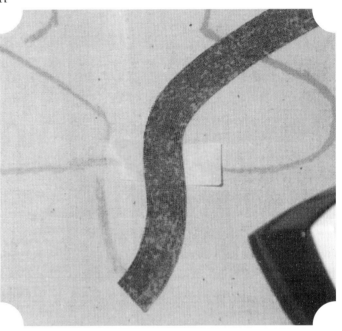

The point is completed to give the appearance of a mitre ..... by trimming the start of the new piece to a point.

This point is laid on top of the previous cord and fused in place.

Always check that there is enough length in a piece of cord to reach the next 'under'. It may be necessary to cut off a substantial piece of cord to end correctly. This can usually be used elsewhere in the design.

Always butt the start of new cords right up against the end of the previous one. Gaps may peep out from under the covering 'over' cord and look unsightly.

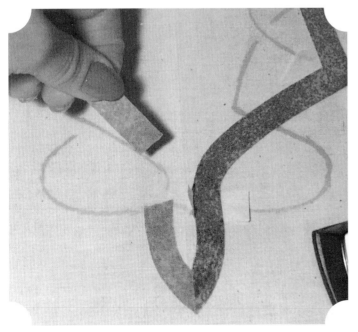

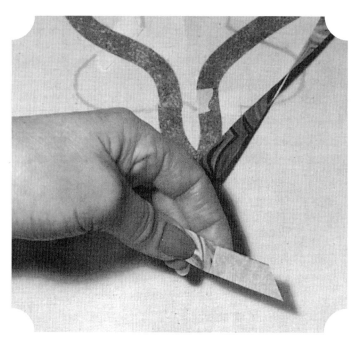

As the fusing progresses weaving the cord under will become necessary.

In order to ease its passage at all 'under' crossings ... re-fuse a short piece of backing paper to the start of the cord.

Trim this to a point. It will now serve as a 'needle' for threading through crossings.

This paper can easily be removed later.

Whenever a cord needs to pass under another, the short paper already inserted should be removed to facilitate the cord's passage.

Because this short paper has been cut from the non stick backing of the fusible web the overlying fabric cord will have temporarily stuck to it. A sharp pull will free it, creating a perfectly sized gap for the 'under' cord to pass through.

The paper point on the 'under' cord will easily poke through this gap to the other side where it can be used to gently pull the rest of the cord into place.

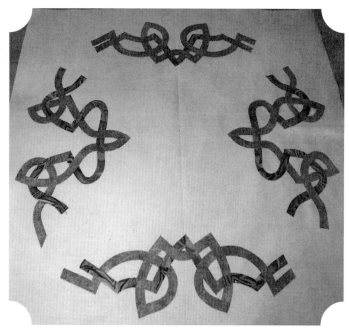

Complete and stitch the cord design before any animals are added.

Stitching is always necessary as the Bondaweb only provides a temporary hold. It is simply acting in the place of pins .....
thousands of them!

(The completed design is shown on page 91.)

20

Stitching Cords

The use of an open toed appliqué foot allows clear visibility in front of the needle.

Both sides of cords should be stitched down by using a very tiny zig zag stitch. This encloses the raw edge of the cord, anchors it in place and prevents fraying.

The machine settings I recommend are ...

stitch width 1·5 ......
stitch length 1 ....

A size 60 /8 machine needle which makes very tiny holes, used with transparent thread, will create near invisible stitching ... a higher sized needle used with decorative thread can also be used to make a feature of the stitching.

When cords cross, one always passes under the other. If this is the one that is being sewn it is necessary to 'jump' over the top cord rather than sewing through it. The 'jump' creates a loop of thread which can be cut away.

To prevent the stitching coming undone at either side of the 'jump' (where it will be cut) return to straight stitching .... and ....

slightly pull the fabric against the action of the feed dog ..... this will progressively shorten the stitch length to nil at the crossing ... creating a 'full stop.'

Lift the presser foot .. jump over the cord and begin to stitch, starting from nil as before. Gently release the pull allowing the stitch length to return to 1 .... alter the stitch width to 1·5 and continue zig zagging around the cord.

Cords can also be made from Quick Bias. In this case the cords will have a folded edge, and a blind hemstitch could be used to sew them down as an alternative to zig zag.

This stitch ......   - - -v- - -v- - -v- - -v

looks very like hand stitching. The straight stitch falls on the backing fabric and the zig zag catches the cord edge.

Use a size 60/8 needle as before with transparent thread (clear on light coloured fabrics and smoke on dark ones) ...... and ...

between ·5 and 1 stitch length and width.

It is not necessary to reduce the stitch length approaching a crossing as these settings produce such a tiny stitch it will not come undone when the loop is cut.

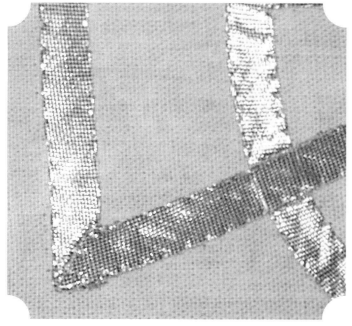

The mitre cut at each cord point also needs to be stitched down .

The raw edge shown here is being zig zagged in the same way as the rest of the cord edge.

The folded mitre created when using Quick Bias should also be sewn down.

It can be easy to miss out stitching a mitre.
To prevent this always stitch all mitres from the same side of a cord ...
e.g. when sewing on the right hand side of a cord remember to stitch all mitres ....
if sewing on the left you can ignore them.

A decorative raised edge can be created by threading a crochet cotton through the central hole in a cording foot and couching the thread in place by using a zig zag stitch.

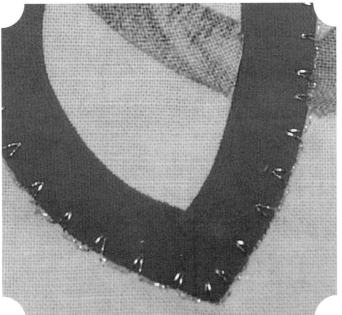

Tie a length of thread around the start of the crochet cotton ... slip the thread through the hole in the front of the machine couching foot .. and it will pull the thicker crochet thread through after it.

A few extra zig zags before doing a 'full stop' at both sides of a crossing will allow the cord to be cut away from over cords.
Metallic crochet cotton looks particularly good.

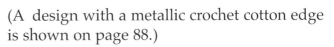

(A design with a metallic crochet cotton edge is shown on page 88.)

Many decorative stitches and threads can add individual touches to any cord.
Be daring and experiment .....

Invisible stitching is certainly not the only option.

Creating Animals

Establish how many copies of which animals you need in any particular design ......
and also if they are mirror images ...
i.e facing in opposite directions.

A tracing must be taken of the outline on freezer paper for each image required.
Always draw on the dull side of freezer paper.

To obtain mirror images ...... fold a piece of freezer paper in half ...... trace one image from the pattern on one half .... trace the second from that tracing on the other half ... through the folded freezer paper.

Draw short lines through all internal lines on all copies. These registration lines will prove very helpful when joining sections together.

Double check that you have not missed any internal lines out ... even if they are short.

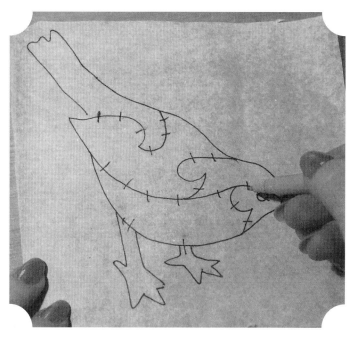

Cut away all surplus paper from around the outside of the animal.

Cut each section apart also.

If making multiple animals it is time saving to cut them all apart at once ... having marked all sections that come from the same animal uniquely
(e.g., same number or coloured pen) ... since the registration points will not match if you mix pieces.

Put all identical sections in a pile on the appropriate fabric chosen ready for ironing.

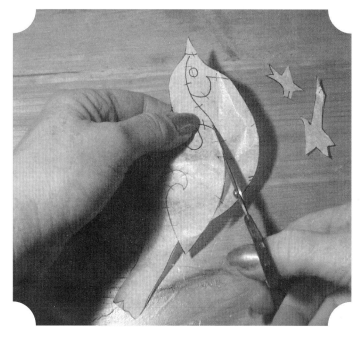

Using a moderately hot dry iron ......
iron each paper section shiny side down on to the **right** side of the chosen fabric.
Leave 1/4 to 1/2in. between pieces.

If the iron is too cool, the paper will be inclined to fall off ....

if too hot the paper will be harder to remove than it need be.

Using scraps of fabric and freezer paper, experiment to find the ideal temperature setting before starting on the actual project.

Cut the fabric allowing a small seam allowance ... approx. 1/8 inch .... around each paper section.

(The technique needs enough allowance to provide a firm hold but not enough to add extra bulk.)

A little experimentation will soon allow you to decide your most comfortable width.

Decide on the first two pieces to be joined. The order does not matter.

Check that the registration marks line up and establish clearly where the join will start and finish.

Every time two pieces are to be joined ... one will have the seam allowance removed so that it can overlap the other ...
and the papers will match edge to edge ... jigsaw puzzle style.

The seam allowance should ideally be cut from the piece containing the darker fabric .... so that it will lie on top. It might show through if it were underneath.

This procedure needs small strips of fusible web. It is essential that the web stays well bonded with its backing paper until you want to separate them.

Bondaweb / Wonder Under / Vliesofix has a tendency for the fusible web to loosen with age and handling. Take the time now to counteract this tendency by following this simple routine.

Cut a piece which will fit onto the teflon ironing sheet, then place both on an ironing board with the fusible side next to the sheet.

Using an iron which is set on a warm setting .. gently iron the two together. This gentle heat will increase the bond between them .

It is a good idea to try this with a small sample first ... to get the iron temperature right. If this is difficult lay a sheet of paper on top to act as insulation.

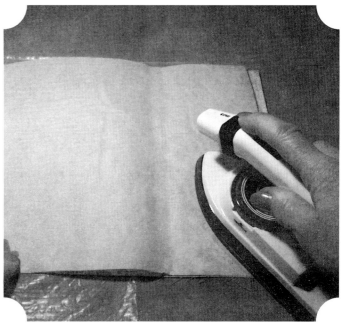

After it has cooled gently peel the fusible from the teflon sheet at one corner .... it should lift easily.

If it sticks ... do not try to pull it away from the sheet .. this will damage the fusible.

Sticking will have been caused by the iron temperature being too hot.

Do not worry ... all is not lost ! ....

we just go to 'plan B'.

Roll the ironing sheet with the Bondaweb still attached.

Place in a freezer for a few minutes . This will make the fusible 'rock hard'.

Try separating the fusible from the sheet again.

Hopefully they will separate easily ...
but if not .. try 'Plan C.'

Lay the sheet and fusible back on the ironing board, and, using a blunt instrument such as the handle of a scissors or rotary cutter ... apply pressure rubbing backwards and forwards over any parts which are stuck. (It does not really matter if it is paper or sheet that is rubbed.)

This action will separate the fusible from the sheet.

If you examine the fusible side you will notice it is shinier than when first bought. This in no way affects its capacity to stick ..... but decreases the chances of separation occurring when it is least desired.

Now you are ready to rotary cut the fusible into narrow strips of 1/4 inch or marginally less.

Bondaweb is at its most vulnerable when in tiny pieces .. so do not cut too many strips at one go.

Cut a few ...... use them as described in the following instructions ...... cut a few more.

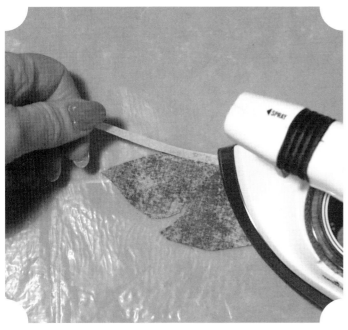

Return to the freezer paper and fabric shapes. Iron a fusible strip to the wrong side of the edge which has had the seam allowance cut from it.

Do this on the non- stick ironing sheet to protect the ironing board.

Allow the fusible to follow the shape of the edge ... tucks which form will not matter.

Make sure that the fusible slightly overlaps the edge. This will help to prevent fraying.

Only apply fusible to the part to be joined.

Flip the piece to the right side and trim away any fusible which overlaps the edge.
This is much easier to do whilst the paper backing is still attached.

Peel away all the paper backing.

Carefully match the paper edges of the pieces to be joined.

The registration lines will enable this to be done with great precision.

When correctly lined up iron the pieces together to bond.

Although this join is only temporary and will be stitched over later to secure ....
it nevertheless forms a stable join which can stand handling without falling apart.

Continue matching and joining pieces in the same way until the animal is complete.

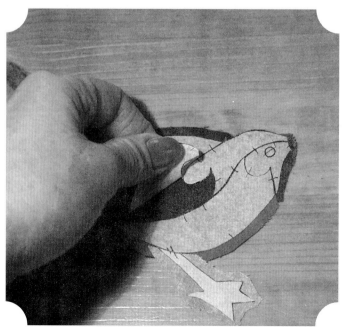

Since freezer paper can be restuck several times it is possible to remove sections to judge the effect ..... but always replace them.

The freezer paper remains in place until the animal is entirely finished and ready to be bonded to the design.

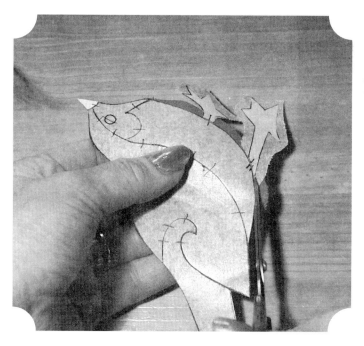

Once all sections of the animal have been joined together trim the allowance from all around the outside edge.

Apply strips of fusible to the wrong side all the way around overlapping the edge as before.

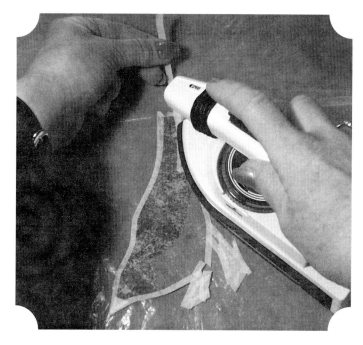

Flip to the right side and trim away surplus fusible.
When you are ready to fuse the animal to the design the paper can be peeled away.

The freezer paper can now be carefully removed.
If paper edges are stuck under fabric edges ... do not pull to release. This would cause fraying.

Instead trim the paper in line with the fabric edge ... the minute amount of paper left under the fabric will not show when the edge is stitched.

Borders can now be added to the finished design before quilting

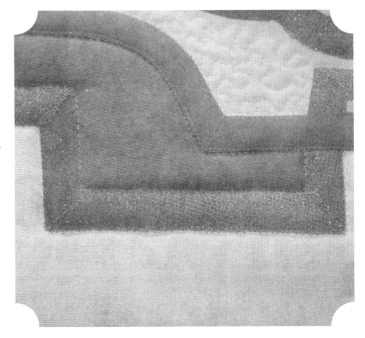

Quilting enhances all patchwork and appliqué.

The interlaced cords provide a great guide for quilting 'in the ditch.'

The cords then become three dimensional.

Spaces between the cords were traditionally of equal importance to the design as the cords themselves.

Important secondary patterns were often placed in spaces.

They provide great opportunities for experimenting with quilting and machine embroidery patterns.

Shown here are examples of contour quilting at different widths (using a walking foot)

and a free machining pattern completed with the feed dogs dropped ...
(using the darning or quilting foot.)

Creating Different Backgrounds
Playing with Squares

Interesting background patterns can be created by joining fabric together by fusing and stitching.

This method has the advantage over traditional seaming, in that wavy or irregular shaped seams can be joined with ease and without bulky seam allowances.

This easy method uses several (e.g. 4) stacked different coloured squares of fabric ....
all right sides uppermost.

Rotary cut a wavy line through all fabrics.

Any of the lower triangles will match with any of the upper triangles to re-form two coloured squares.

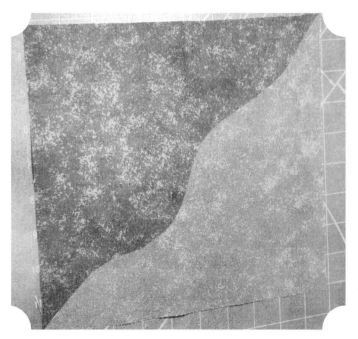

These can be seamed together by fusing and zig zag stitching.

The squares can be joined together at this stage ....

or .....

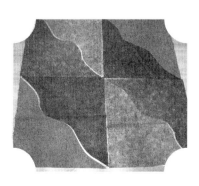

33

The two coloured squares can be stacked once more .....

and rotary cut once again ....
in another wavy line.

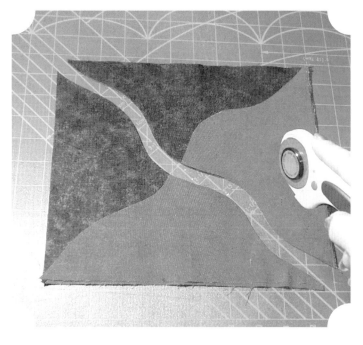

All lower triangles can be mixed with upper triangles to create new four coloured squares ...

which will create new patterns when joined together.

Celtic cords can then be superimposed on top.

(Examples with this kind of background are shown on pages 82 and 86.)

Fun with Cords

Many quilters are attracted to hand dyeing or painting fabric .... only to put the results away in a drawer because they were not sure what to do with them.

This is the moment that hand dyed fabric has has been waiting for ....

It looks marvellous cut into bias strips for Celtic cords. The colours come and go, blending beautifully around a design.

(Check out 'Fabulous Feathers' on page 82.)

Manufactured Quick Bias now comes in many colours including wonderful metallics.

Celtic cords can be made entirely in these ....
or a mixture of cut fabric and Quick Bias.

It can be used on the designs at the size provided or ....

photocopy the designs reduced by 20% which will give a more compact appearance.

Quick Bias examples ......
'Dragon flight' on page 82, '
and 'Fish Tail' on page92.

Don't forget to consider striped or patterned fabrics for creating cords.

Be prepared for a surprise when heavily patterned fabric is cut into bias strips.
The results are often unpredictable ...
especially when mixing colours.
Two fabrics which look worlds apart in the whole cloth can look similar when stripped in narrow widths.

Check out the contrasting border fabrics in 'Celtic Glitz' on page 85.
These are the same two fabrics that are bias cut for the cords. Their colour difference has almost disappeared.

Colour Sequenced Cords

Using similar toned ... or ... contrasting coloured fabric in a predetermined colour sequence can be fun to do and give pleasing and spectacular results.

First ..... decide how many colours you wish to use. (Three and seven were numbers with special significance for the Celts.)

Next ..... decide in which order they look good. Number fabrics ... (if only in your head.)

Prepare some of each fabric as previously described .... and bias cut at your chosen width.

Apply the bias to the marked pattern using one ..... or both of the following rules ...

Change colour at all under crossings.

Change colour at all points.

The colour changes should follow the chosen sequence ..and then reverse it ... returning to the beginning .... e.g., 1 2 3 4 5 6 5 4 3 2 1
It really does not matter if the mirror images of designs are not exact matches.

As long as the colour sequence is maintained, it will look great.

(When nearing the end of the design ...
i.e., approaching the place where you started ... it may be necessary to miss every alternate colour in the sequence to return you speedily to the first number in line with the start.

This strategy will be less noticible than number 6 linking with number 1.)

Points can look three dimensional in two colours.
(See examples on pages 82, 83, 86, 90 and 91.)

Strip Pieced Cords

Another way to achieve a new look with cords is to strip piece different fabrics together before cutting them into bias strips.

Choose the number ...
    the widths ....
        the colours ....
            the order ....

of the fabrics that you wish to use.

Stagger each fabric approx 2 ¹/₂ in. from the end of its neighbour. (the measurement will vary according to the chosen strip width .... check the exact amount by placing the ruler across the fabric as if you were about to cut it at 45°

This will eliminate wastage when cutting.

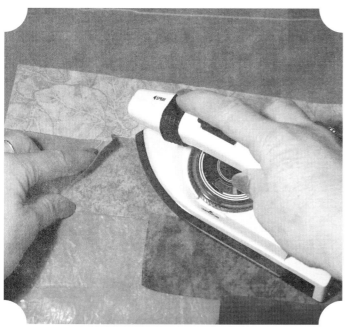

Join them together by overlapping and fusing as already explained on page.

Using this method in preference to traditional seaming eliminates all the seam allowances on the wrong side of the fabric.

When cut on the bias there will be no problem with fabric points peeping out from underneath as the cords travel around bends.

Zig zag to secure .... over the raw edges throughout the length of each seam.

Decorative stitching over the invisible zig zag can add colour and interest.

Many automatic machine stitches and glitzy threads combine well for this purpose.

Apply Bondaweb to the back of the stripped fabric before rotary cutting into bias strips.

Use in the same way as previously described to complete the cord design.

See pages 83 and 88 for strip pieced examples.

Creating Coloured Inserts

The importance of spaces in traditional Celtic design has already been mentioned.

Another way of enhancing these areas in needleworked designs is to introduce another fabric to fill selected spaces.

This is easy to do by cutting out the fabric from the chosen space using the cord line as a cutting guide.

Cut out and fill each space one at a time to avoid weakening the background fabric.

Turn the background fabric to the wrong side and fuse a Bondaweb strip around the edge of the hole ... overlapping the edge.

Return the fabric to the right side and trim away the excess fusible.

Peel away the backing paper.

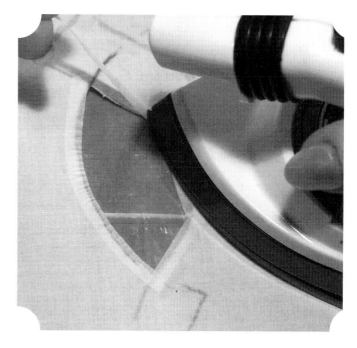

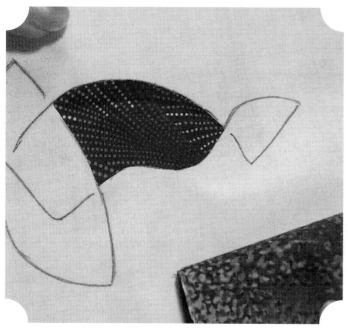

Possible fabric choices can be auditioned by holding then behind the hole.

Glitzy Lurex and other metallic fabrics can look great!.

(See 'Celtic Glitz' on page 85.)

Use the cut out fabric shape as a pattern ..... cutting the new filler fabric approx. 1/8 in. bigger all around.

On the wrong side ... position the filler fabric over the hole ... right side down.

Iron to fuse in place.

Repeat at each selected hole until all have been filled.

(Neighbouring holes are no trouble to fill .... if they are done one at a time.)

No stitching is necessary at this stage .

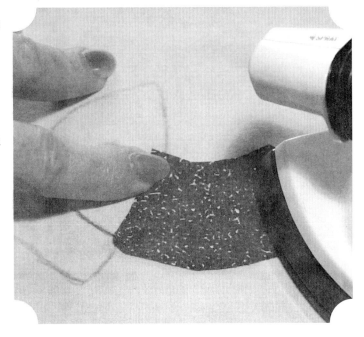

Fusing and stitching the bias cords in the usual way will anchor all filler fabrics securely in place ....

as will quilting in the ditch at a later stage.

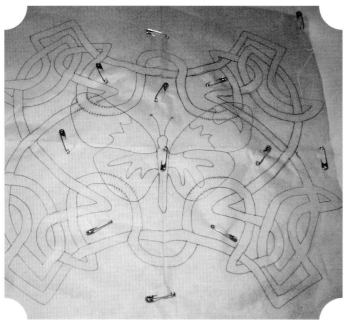

Quilted Celtics.

Celtic patterns can also look great as quilted designs ... either hand or machine stitched on plain fabric. For the fastest most efficient way to a machine quilted Celtic design ......
trace the pattern as described ...
mark the 'unders and overs' ....
superimpose an animal if you wish
place the tracing paper on top of the three layers .... top fabric .... batting/wadding ... and backing fabric .....
pinning together through all three layers.
(Cord lines which fall within the butterfly's wings have been crossed out as they will not be quilted.)

Stitch along the lines through paper and all layers ....

using either the standard presser foot with the feed dog raised for normal stitching ...

or .....

the darning or embroidery foot and the feed dogs lowered ...... allowing free motion stitching.

Quilting can be completed in either transparent or coloured thread.

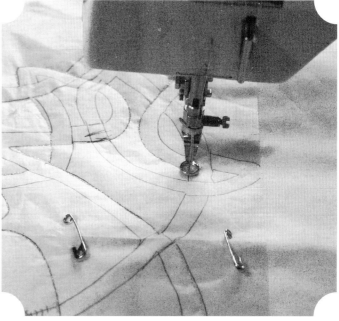

Tear away the tracing paper when the stitching is finished

Quilted colour and texture can also be added by filling the cords or spaces with free machining

e.g., small 'beads' of satin stitch add both colour and texture.

See machine quilted example of butterfly on page 93 ......

and a beautiful example of hand quilted swans inside the back cover.

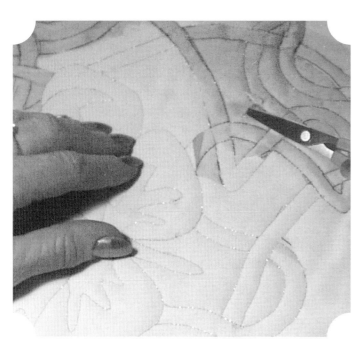

41

Patterns for Butterflies, Birds and Beasties.
(Instructions page 23)

Think of each of these patterns as a "painting by numbers" picture.

Each separate section in the picture can be filled with a different colour fabric.

Designs can be simplified by omitting some of the internal lines.

Designs can be individualised by replacing all of the internal lines with your own version.

It is not essential to use realistic creature colouring .... but you can if you wish.

Eyes can be appliquéd as per the instructions ..... indicated by beads ... embroidered ....

or drawn in using permanent pen. .

Resizing by photocopying ... or reversing the creature direction may better suit individual projects.

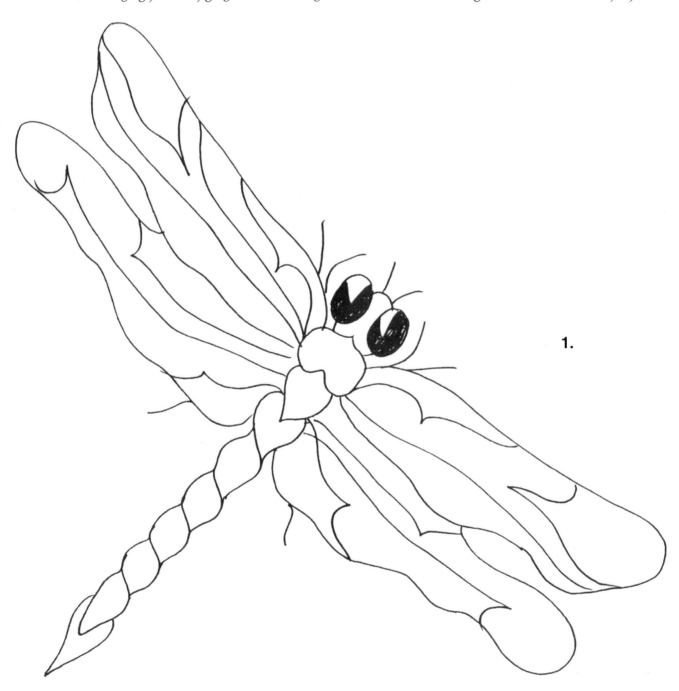

1.

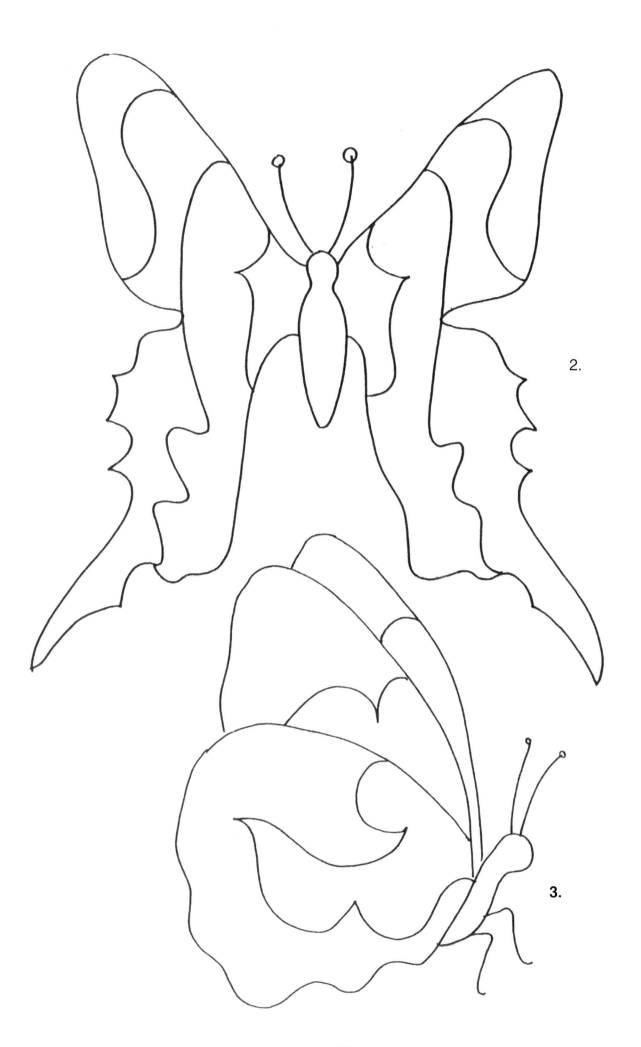

2.

3.

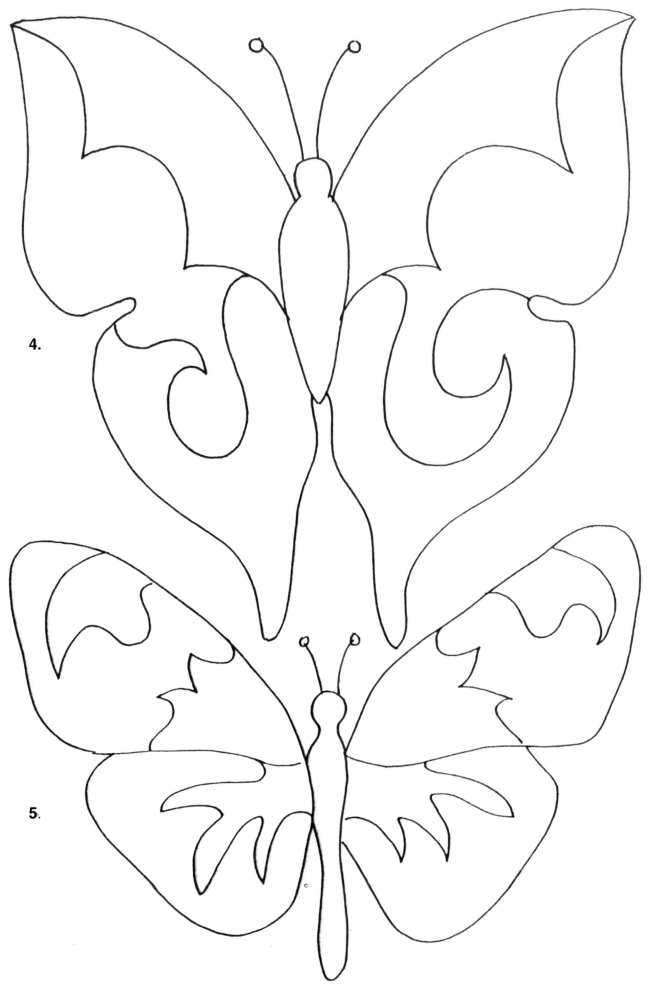

4.

5.

6.

7.

8.

9.

10.

11

12.

13.

14.

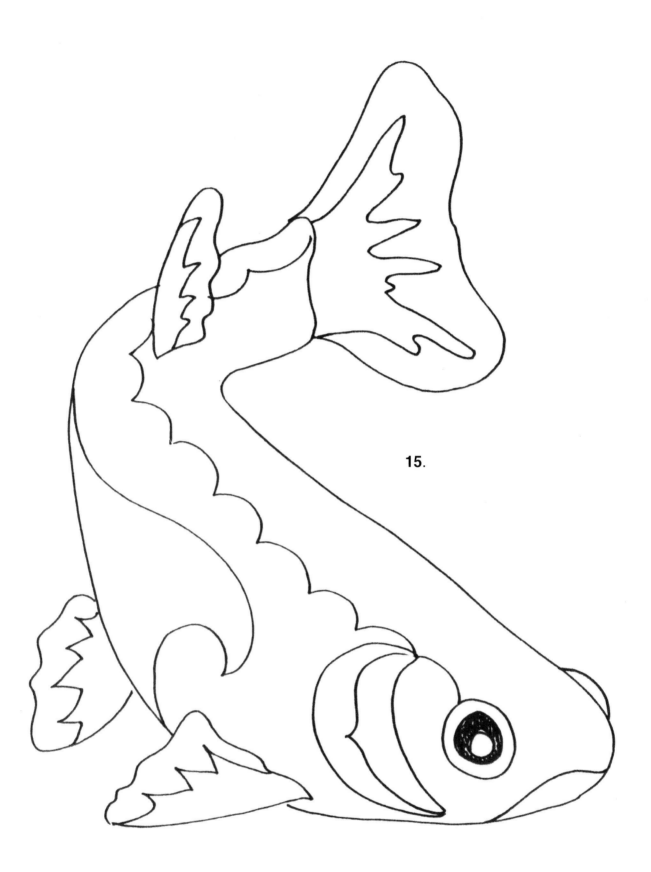

15.

27.

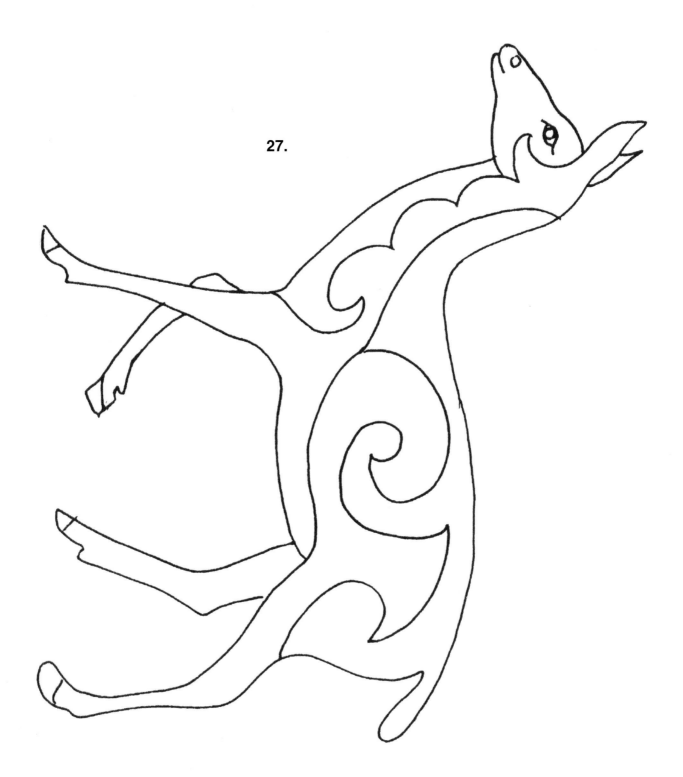

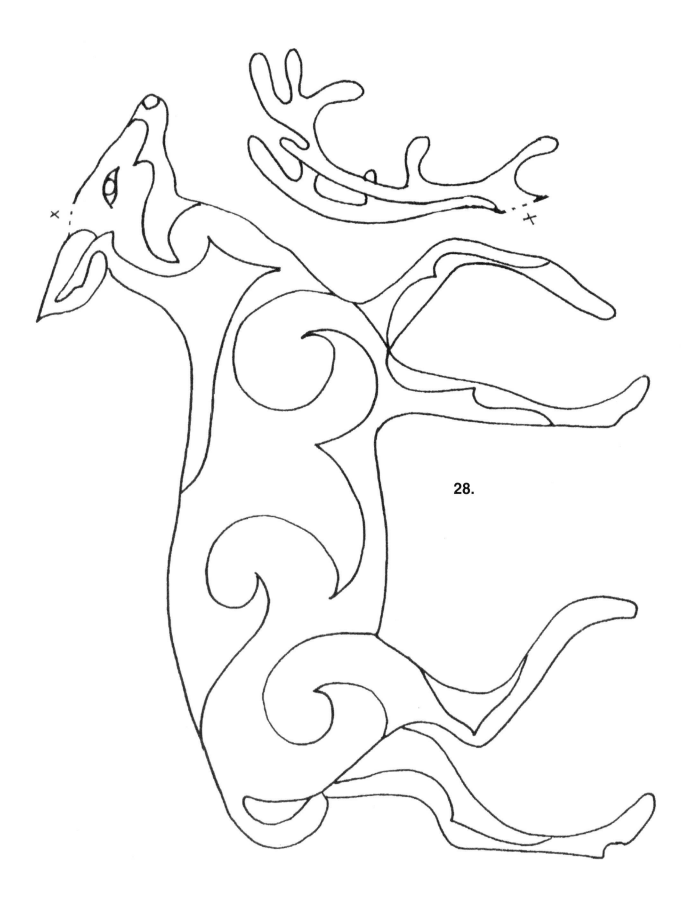

28.

29.

30.

38.

39.

40.

41.

42.

43.

44.

45.

50.

51.

52.

53.

54.

55.

56.

57.

58.

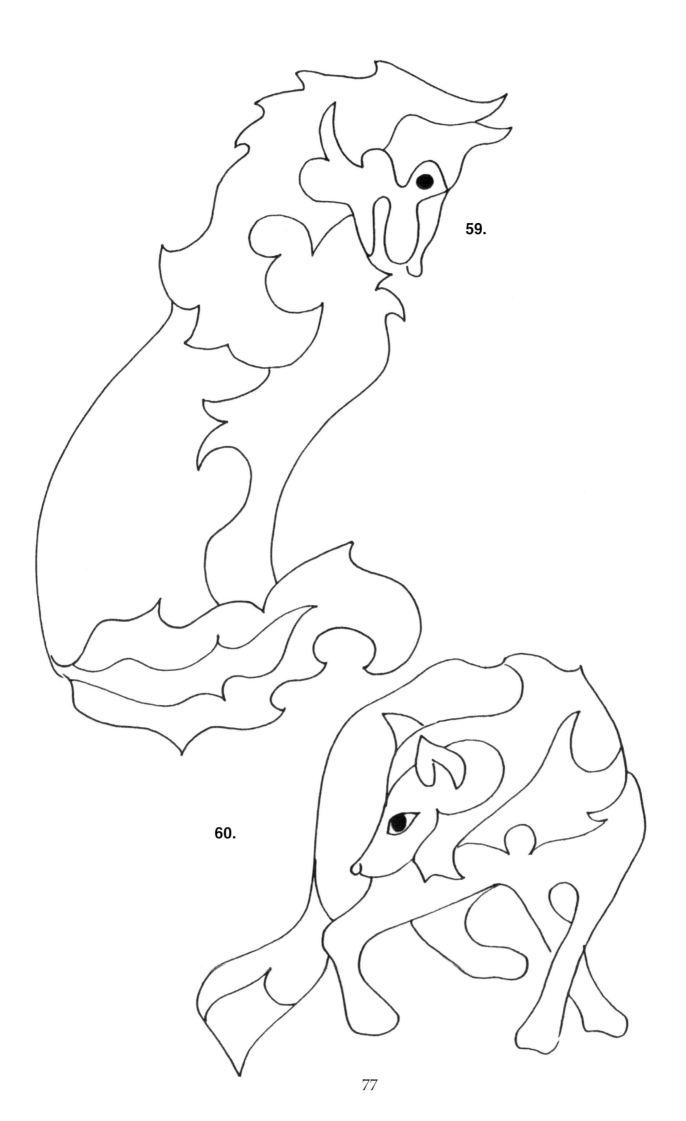

59.

60.

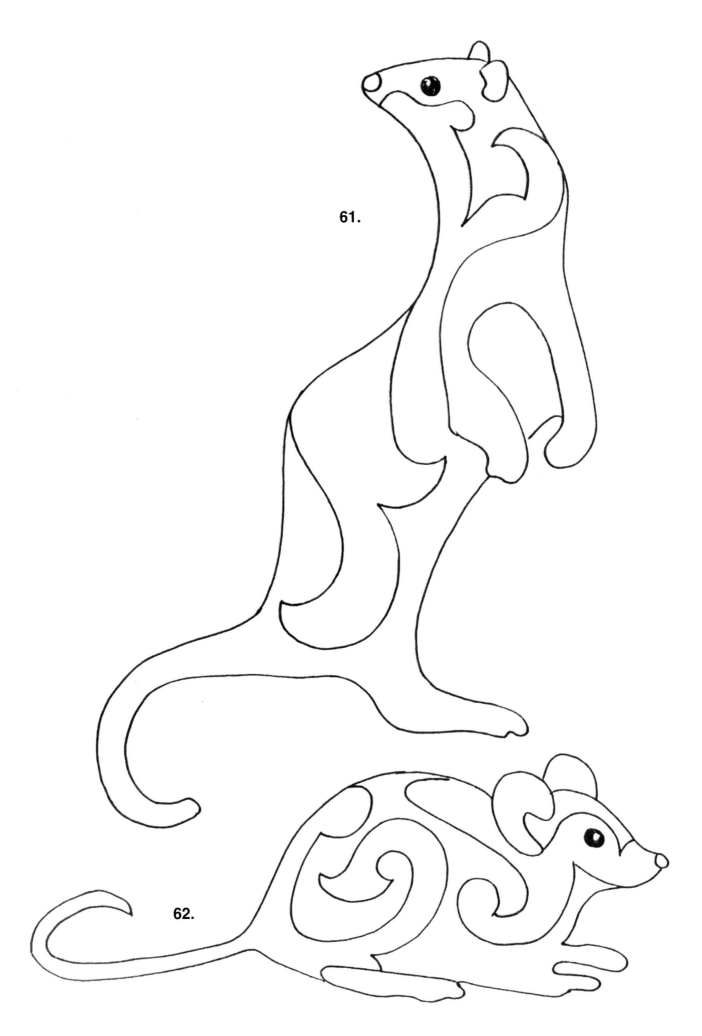

61.

62.

63

64.

'Christmas is coming'

a Celtic Advent calender...(with removable decorations)

by Alison King.

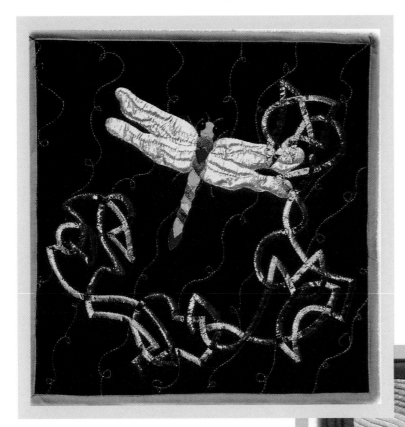

'Dragonfly'
by
the author.

Quick Bias cords.
pattern no.1. p.42

'Celtic Cotton
Patch'
by
the author.

Colour sequenced cords.

'Fabulous
Feathers'
by
the author.

Hand dyed cords.
pattern no.36. p.62.

82

'I'm a Peartree quilter'
by
Sue Martin.

colour sequenced cords.
Pattern no.29. p.58.

'Now you see it ... now you don't'
by
the author.

Strip pieced cords.

'Where's 'e gone?'
by
Sue Martin.

Two different coloured cords.
Patterns nos. 41 & 62. p. 66 & 78.

(Two different coloured cords)

'Celtic Glitz'
by
Jane Plowman.

'Over, under and out'
by
Carmen Redler.

(colour sequence cords)
Pattern no.5. p. 44.

'Celtic Illusion'
by
the author

two different coloured fabric
cords.

'The eagle has landed'
by
Sue Martin

(Hand dyed cords)

Pattern no.37. p.63.

'Corded Celtic'

by

the author

(Strip pieced cords.)

'On Celtic pond'

by

the author.

(Single fabric cords.) Patterns nos.13 & 14. p.48.

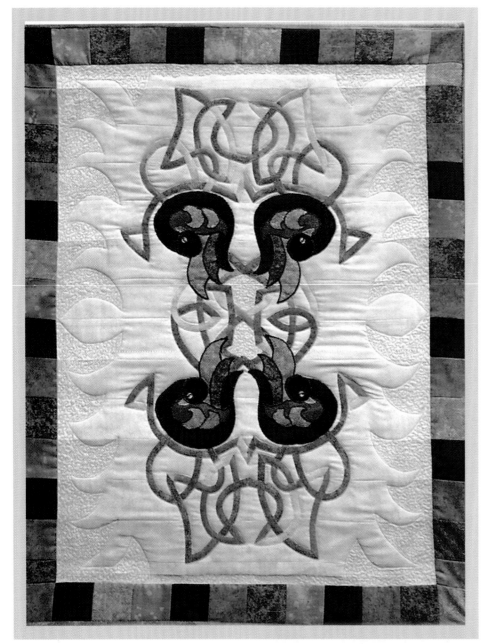

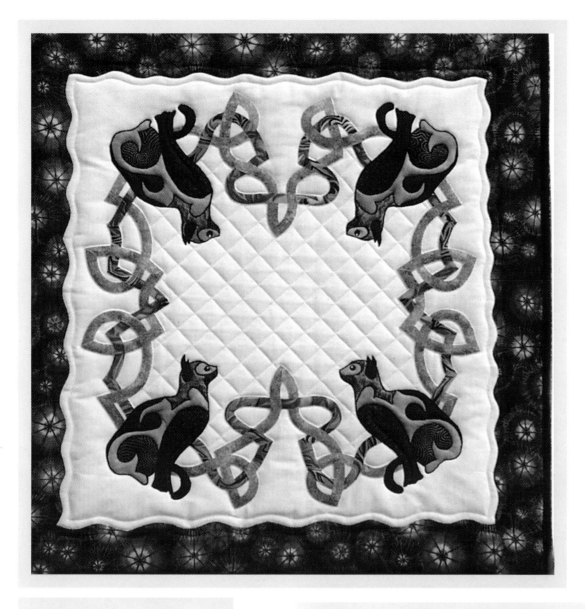

91

'A Fishy Tail'
by
the author.

(Quick Bias cords.)
Pattern no.16. p.50.

'Rich Chicks'
by
Mary Rich.

(Colour sequenced cords.)
Patterns nos.44 & 45.
p.68 & 69.

(Two different coloured cords.)

Pattern no.40. p.65.

'Celtic Flight'
and
machine embroidered
butterfly.
Both by the author.

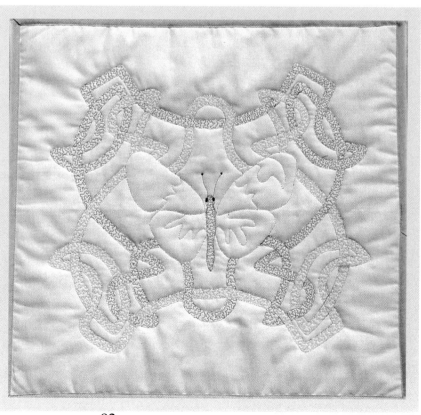

Pattern no.5 p.44.

(Hand dyed cords)
Pattern no.5. p. 44.

(Quick Bias cords.) Pattern no.58. p. 76.

94

Angela Madden's unique books and tools ....
very clever techniques and very clear instructions.

'Sew Easy Celtic'..... A truly unique and easy way to design your own original Celtic knotwork patterns for needlework and other crafts. Absolutely no artistic or mathematical skill needed for brilliant, fast, machine sewn results. Based on drawing symmetrical doodles .... so anyone can do it ! If you've ever cut out a paper snowflake you can do this.

'Magic Celtic'............ More easy designing ... this time using the 'Circle Slice ruler' to draft accurate wedge shaped slices, and more doodles, to create multi - sectional knotwork designs .... they look amazingly complicated ... but are easy to draft and fast to machine sew.

'Appliqué and Roses'............ An appliqué block and border design technique. This book shows how to easily create limitless original patterns. Fast machine sewing. The same principles can also be applied to drafting vine designs ..... with a new, fast multiple production system for adding 3D roses and leaves. Forget copying other peoples patterns ... be original ..... create your own in half the time!

'Slice up a Circle'............ easy "geometricks" for patchworkers create wonderful original star, compass, and kaleidoscopic designs. Use the 'Circle Slice ruler' again for easy accuracy. With freezer paper everything fits together like a jig saw puzzle, and it's easy to add curves without any tricky curved seam piecing.

'Pieceful Scenes'........ gives the traditional blocks of your choice a brand new look by linking them with a landscape in a three dimensional illusion. If you can draw a straight line using a pencil and a ruler you already have all the skills required to draft your own original 3D designs. Freezer paper piecing facilitates fast, trouble free assembly.

'Paradise Flowers'........... the ultimate book of floral design ...... a unique and easy way to design and machine sew original flower patterns ..... traditional style or as 'different' as you choose to make them ... any size for any project. As usual no artistic ability is required for brilliant results. One pattern on its own looks good ... but assemble them in multiples in different combinations and they look amazing! Patterns can be used for patchwork. quilting, a new method of 'stained glass' stencilling, embroidery or trapunto. Design a flower and create a garden !

'Photo Fabrications'....... easy machine appliqué from family photos .... the easiest way ever to achieve true appliqué copies of landscapes ... pets ... houses ... people ..... in fact whatever you wish. No artistic talent required for stunning results ... just a little courage to have a go ... the ability to trace and zig zag stitch and the crucial 'know how.'
Great for gifts ... or recording special events.

Tools ....

The 'Circle Slice Ruler'..... takes all the inaccuracy out of drafting precise angles for multi - sectional designing .... none of the problems of using a protractor !
Essential for' Magic Celtic' and 'Slice up a Circle' and an optional extra to extend the possibilities of 'Paradise Flowers'

The ' Multi - Plait' Tool ..... a unique tool which facilitates the drafting of plaits (braids) quickly and accurately in different styles and sizes. The patterns created are suitable for quilting, embroidery, appliqué or bias appliqué, for both block and border designs using varying numbers of cords. It is really easy to understand and speedy to use ...... and it takes plaits correctly around corners for you too!. Creates ideal borders to accompany Celtic designs.

The 'Feather Tool'.... traditional feathered wreathes, borders, hearts, squares etc. are universally popular designs. This original tool is the essential aid to fast drafting ... feather any shape and in any size.

Video.

'Creative Celtic ' .... made in conjunction with Nancy Zieman's U.S. Public T.V.'s program host of 'Sewing with Nancy' In this video I explain and demonstrate my unique Celtic design techniques showing and discussing many examples of my work.

'Paradise Flowers' ..... this video (also made with Nancy Zieman) follows the techniques from my book of the same name. Again the techniques are fully explained and demonstrated with many examples of my own and my students work.
Each of the above videos covers three programmes from Nancy's very popular show.

Videos are available by mail order only from....

Nancy's Notions. 333 Beichl Ave. P.O. Box 683. Beaver Dam. WI. 53916-0683. U.S.A.
Tel U.S.A. 1-800-833-0690. Fax 1-800-255-8119.
Web Site. nancysnotions.com

Angela Madden's website .... angelamadden.com.

For current details of workshops and talks/slide lectures please send S.A.E. marked 'workshops' to the publication address on page 1. (U.K. or abroad)

Last..... but definitely not least .....

should you feel inspired to make an item using the instructions in this ......
or any other of my books ...... please send a photo to the publication address on page 1.
Not only would I personally love to see your work ....
all my future students would love to see it too ......
that's how ideas multiply and enthusiasm is spread.